People of the Longhouse

FIREFLY BOOKS

People of the Longhouse

How the Iroquoian Tribes Lived

Jillian & Robin Ridington

Illustrations by Ian Bateson

A FIREFLY BOOK

For our mothers, Ida Botham and Edith Farr
Ridington, who taught us our first lessons
and guide us still.

Copyright © Jillian Ridington and Robin Ridington, 1982
Illustrations copyright © Ian Bateson, 1982
First paperback edition 1992
First published in Canada by:
Douglas & McIntyre

This edition published in the
United States in 1995 by:

Firefly Books (U.S.) Inc.
P.O. Box 1325
Ellicott Station
Buffalo, N.Y.
14205

Cataloguing in Publication Data

Ridington, Jillian, 1936-
    People of the longhouse : how the Iroquoian
tribes lived

(How they lived in Canada)
ISBN 1-55054-221-4

1. Iroquoian Indians—Juvenile literature.
I. Ridington, Robin, 1939-   . II. Title
III. Series.

E99.I69R53 1992   970.004'97   C92-093992-9

Book design by Ian Bateson
Typesetting by Domino-Link Graphic
Communications Ltd.
Printed and bound in Canada by
D.W. Friesen & Sons Ltd.

Contents

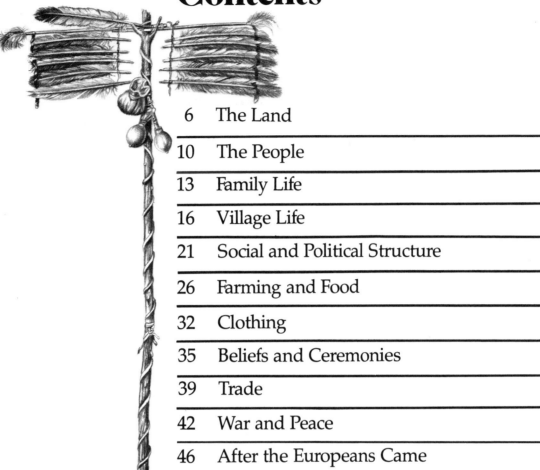

The Land

Long before Europeans came to this continent, Indians grew crops along a "corn belt" that stretched from Georgian Bay on Lake Huron south to Mexico, where the techniques and tools for growing corn, squash and beans originated about 5000 years ago. The northernmost of these native peoples, the Iroquoians, were Canada's first cultivators. They lived around the southern Great Lakes and in the St. Lawrence River valley, where the land was fertile and easy to work without metal tools.

Maize, as Indian corn was called, required 120 days without frost to ripen. Beyond Georgian Bay, the rocky soil and long winters made it impossible to grow maize. In the land of the Iroquoians, four well-marked seasons divided the agricultural year. Spring was a time of flowing sap and new buds. The earth thawed and was easily worked, ready to receive seed. Summer was dry, warm and long. July temperatures ranged in the twenties degrees Celsius. Before the corn was ripe, strawberries, raspberries and wild cherries could be gathered.

Autumn was a time of brilliant colours. The corn stalks turned from green to buff. The maple, birch and beech leaves blazed red and gold. Orange pumpkins and squash coloured the ground. Women harvested them together with the corn, late-ripening blackberries and sweet crab apples. In winter, the snow was deep. The

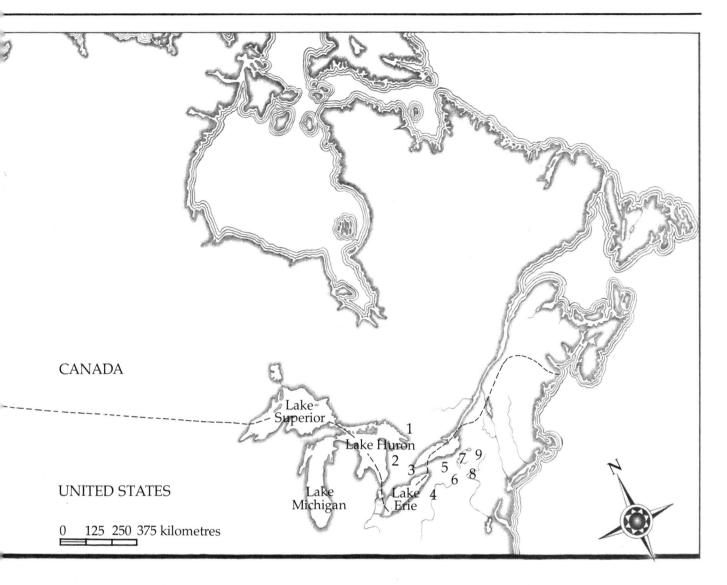

CANADA

Lake
Superior

1

Lake Huron

2

UNITED STATES

3   5   7 9
         8
        6

Lake
Michigan

Lake
Erie   4

0   125 250 375 kilometres

N

Woman using a husking pin to remove the kernels from the cob of a fresh ear of corn. In front of her are some other plants that Iroquoians cultivated: pumpkins, squash, marrows and a variety of beans.

IROQUOIAN-SPEAKING GROUPS

1. Huron League	2. Petun (or Tobacco) League
3. Neutral League	4. Erie

League of the Iroquois

5. Seneca	6. Cayuga
7. Onondaga	8. Oneida
9. Mohawk	

Huron trading party disembarking from its Algonkian birchbark canoes which are heavily loaded with baskets and clay pots full of dried meat, furs, clothing and ornaments

rivers and smaller lakes, frozen beneath the drifts, blended into the land. January temperatures averaged just below freezing. In this season of cold, people stayed close to their longhouse fires or travelled short distances by snowshoe.

No steep mountains divided the land. The birch, hemlock and pine of the northern forest blended into the maple, elm, ash and beech of the eastern woodlands. Gentle hills, easily climbed, provided high

points from which to spot an enemy or watch for returning kinsmen. Near such hills, and close to rivers or lakes where soil was sandy and water easily available, the Iroquoians built their villages.

The Great Lakes and hundreds of smaller lakes are joined by a network of rivers. Iroquoian men paddled these natural highways in bark canoes. These craft carried cargoes of corn, beans and animal skins to trade with friendly neighbours, or warriors intent on raiding enemy villages.

The fertile land made the Iroquoian way of life possible. Without their crops, the Iroquoians would have had to rely on hunting to feed themselves. Hunting people must follow their food supply and must devote most of their time to the pursuit of game. Farmers can grow their food in the same place year after year and can establish settled villages. Since women did the farming to produce the basic foods, Iroquoian men were free to travel, to trade and to raid.

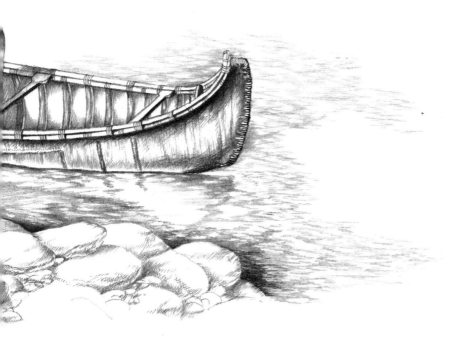

The People

For about 1000 years, the culture and languages of the Iroquoians dominated the central northeastern woodlands. These people spoke closely related Iroquoian languages, but each tribe had its own way of speaking and its own special customs.

The Iroquoians thought of their tribes as separate nations. The League of the Iroquois was called the Five Nations because it was made up of the Mohawk, Oneida, Onondaga, Seneca and Cayuga tribes. "Iroquois" was the name they were called by their enemies, the Ojibwa — and it means "poisonous snakes," but the five nations called each other by their tribal names in their own languages. At the time of its greatest strength, the League of the Iroquois had about 10 000 members.

The Bear, Cord, Rock and Deer nations who made up the Huron League lived in Huronia, the peninsula of land on the southeast corner of Lake Huron's Georgian Bay. The French called these people "Huron" which means "unkempt knave." The Huron preferred to be called "Wendat" which means "dwellers of the peninsula." With a population of between 20 000 and 30 000, the Huron formed the largest and most powerful of all the Iroquoian leagues. Although each nation had its own villages, they were close together, and all members of the Huron League hunted the forest between settlements.

South of Huronia and to the west were the lands of the Tobacco (or Petun) and the

Iroquoian adults loved children and were not strict with them; boys and girls were rarely punished and thought it a great disgrace just to be scolded

Neutral leagues. Although the soil in this southern area was not quite as easily worked as it was in Huronia, the climate was warmer. Tobacco thrived, and fruits and berries were abundant.

Farther to the southwest were the lands of the Erie or Cat people, so called because they often wore the skins of the bobcats that abounded in their territory. The Erie were the only Iroquoians not organized into a league.

The Neutral and Erie lived in the warmest part of Iroquoian territory, where the growing season was longest and the greatest variety of crops could be grown. They had the most people for the size of the lands they occupied. However, the total population of the Huron was greater because they had a lot more territory.

Although the Five Nations people were very like the Huron in many ways, members of the two leagues were enemies. This was, in part, simply because Iroquoian men saw raiding and warfare as the means of demonstrating their courage and proving their worth. Another reason was competition for trade routes.

In appearance, the Iroquoians were strong and lithe. They were taller than most Europeans at the time the two peoples first met. Because they had no written language, people developed excellent memories. They could remember long stories and speeches, and repeat them word for word even years after hearing them. The Iroquoians valued self-reliance, endurance and courage in both men and women. They could be cruel to their enemies but were gentle and considerate within their own groups.

Co-operation among those who lived in the same house, village or nation was essential. Each person knew that the group had to work together in order to survive. During the growing season, scouts and sentries were always present, because an enemy attack could endanger the food supply. In the biggest villages, groups of over 1000 people were able to live together, far more than could do so in nomadic hunting bands. These big groups could engage in elaborate ceremonies and games. They could also work together to build the huge longhouses in which they lived.

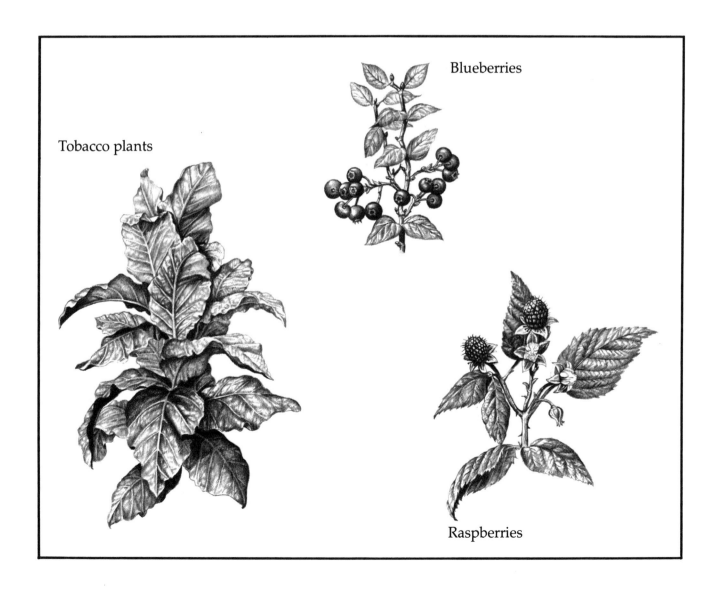

Blueberries

Tobacco plants

Raspberries

Family Life

Each Iroquoian longhouse was home to many families. These families were related to each other through their female members, since all children born to the women of a longhouse became members of a kin group called a clan. A clan was made up of people who could trace their descent through their mothers and grandmothers back to a common female ancestor. Male and female clan members of the same age group thought of themselves as being like brothers and sisters.

Every tribe had a number of clans, named for animals that were important to the people, such as the bear, wolf, turtle or hawk. A large clan might fill several houses in a village. The clan was headed by the clan matron, the oldest, most respected woman in it. She controlled the food supply, selected chiefs and arranged marriages for clan members.

In some tribes, a man's mother suggested a possible wife to him. If he liked her choice, she would speak to the woman's mother, who would then decide whether or not the man was a skilled enough hunter and warrior to marry her daughter.

Even after marriage, a woman's bonds to her clan were more important than her tie to her husband. Her world was centred on the longhouse and fields where she lived and worked with her mother and sisters. Any children born to her would belong to her clan. Children were always

The clan matron had a strong influence over life in the long-house. She controlled the food supply, selected chiefs and arranged marriages. Since a clan was thought of as a large family, marriage partners had to come from a different clan.

raised by their mother and her sisters and brothers, not by their father. Although a man moved into the longhouse of his wife's clan after marriage, he still spent a great deal of his time with his own clan, helping to raise the children of his sisters. Because a man's world was centred on the woods and waterways, he was often away from the village.

Childbirth proved a woman's competence and courage, just as success in battle proved a man's. She gave birth alone or with the help of an experienced older woman. If she cried or made noise during labour, she was considered cowardly and was scolded for setting a bad example.

The birth of a girl was greeted with joy, because she could give birth to more clan members and so ensure its strength. When a boy was born he was dipped into a stream right away; this was supposed to make him strong and fearless. Every baby was given a taste of animal oil right after birth to clean out his or her system. It also fed the child's guardian spirit which was believed to live in the soul from birth on.

Children had special names that identified them as belonging to a particular clan. The mother chose the name from a list of those owned by her clan and not being used by any living person. The child's name was confirmed at the next major festival.

As children grew up, they learned how to do things by watching and imitating the work of adults. When they were strong enough, toddlers helped to fetch wood and water. They carried the water in small pots that held about 500 mL. The pots looked like vases and were made of clay mixed with pounded stone or shells for strength.

Girls learned to make pots by forming very little ones which they used as toys. They rolled the wet clay mixture into a ball, then made a dent in this with a fist. To shape the pot, they slapped the outside with a wooden paddle, while turning the pot on their fist. The pots were dried in the sun, then baked in a hot fire. Iroquoians did not glaze their pots, but they did press patterns into the rims with corncobs, fingernails and other objects.

Girls were also taught how to pound dried corn into corn meal. They moved stout wooden pestles up and down in a mortar made from a hollowed-out tree trunk which was filled with dried corn.

Boys practised archery and other skills that would help develop their co-ordination, sharp sight and good aim to make them useful in the woods and warfare. They also learned to fish and snare animals by copying the men. At puberty, most boys went on a vision quest. They spent about two weeks in the forest, alone and without food, waiting for their guardian spirit to show itself. The spirit would foretell their future and give them a special song. Singing the song would give them courage and protect them in times of danger.

When girls reached puberty they cooked and ate their food alone, using special pots. Throughout their childbearing years, women observed these practices at each menstrual period.

Not all members of a clan were born into it. Adoption of both children and adults was common. In wartime, when many men were killed, clan matrons could adopt enemy captives so that their groups remained strong.

For the first year, a baby spent its waking hours in a cradleboard and was taken everywhere in it. The board could be propped against the wall of a house or hung from a tree near the women as they worked, or carried on the back of the baby's mother, sister or aunt. Cattail fluff served as diapers. At night the baby slept with its parents or in a hammock made of animal skins.

Village Life

Because the Iroquoian people were farmers, they did not have to move from place to place like the hunting people of the northern forest. Instead, they lived in villages near their fields. Large villages had palisades made of three rows of slender poles more than twice the height of a man. The poles were placed a few centimetres apart, reinforced with bark slabs, then woven together with branches. At the top were watchtowers, from which sentries kept a lookout. The palisades had only a single opening to make sneak attacks difficult. When tribe members in smaller villages were threatened, they took shelter in the fortified villages.

Villages had to be moved every 10 to 20 years, because the soil became worn out from farming and supplies of wood got used up. The new site was located as close as possible to the old one. The young men cleared the land and built new longhouses. House sites were in a random pattern so that fires could not spread easily.

Iroquoian homes were called longhouses because of their shape. They were often 40 m or more in length and 10 m in width. A village could have as many as 30 longhouses, with as many as 100 people living in each. At each corner of the building, the Iroquois used posts up to 10 cm across, sunk about a metre into the ground, with smaller posts in between. Perhaps 4 m above the ground, each corner post was notched to hold the four main

Inside a longhouse, the woman in the back is using a sieve made of hickory wood to sift the ashes out of kernels of popped corn. The woman to the right is grinding dried corn on a mortar in preparation for a meal. In the front, a mother is teaching her young daughter the art of pottery.

Men playing lacrosse. Lacrosse sticks were about 160 cm long and were made of wood; at the top was a basket woven from leather thongs. The balls were carved from wood or made of deerhide stuffed with hair.

cross beams. Slender poles were placed across the beams to form a framework for the roof. The sides were covered with overlapping large pieces of bark cut like boards, held in place by splints and rope made from bark. The front and back had openings which were fitted with bark doors set on wooden hinges, or hung with a bear or deer skin. Roof shingles were made of thinner pieces of bark. Holes were drilled in them so they could be attached to the roof frame with bark-fibre thongs. In the centre of the roof was an opening to allow smoke to escape, and light to enter.

Huron longhouses were similar. They had longer poles tied together at the top to form the roof. This gave their houses a more rounded shape. Also, Huron houses were tapered at each end and had storage porches inside the doorways.

In all homes, a long aisle ran down the centre, and cooking fires were made in this space. Along each side wall were rooms for each family, set apart by partitions made of hide or bark. Each family had its own metre-high sleeping or sitting platform, under which was stored food and utensils. For sleeping, bear skins were placed on top of it. Above the platforms were high lofts in which to store food supplies.

When people got together for a festival, the clans who shared each village played games and sports against each other. Lacrosse, now Canada's national sport, was invented by the Iroquois, who believed their ancestors gave them the game to develop the endurance and agility to become great warriors. Players raced the length of the field, using their sticks to carry the ball, to throw and catch passes, and to fling the ball into the goal. In summer, teams of men from different clans, villages or even nations played long, hard-fought games on grassy fields beside villages. For the big games held during major festivals, each team had hundreds of men.

In winter, they played snowsnake. It was usually a boy's game, but men played snowsnake as a team sport. They slid curved sticks over the snow to hit a wooden ball.

Winter was also the time for making and repairing clothes, goods and tools. The Five Nations made canoes from elm bark. They took large pieces of bark off a tree and removed the rough outside layer. Then they joined the pieces to form a canoe, pointed at both ends. A rim of ash wood strips was run around the edge, outside and in, and tied in place with bark twine. Ribs were also made of ash, set into the canoe at 20-cm intervals and secured under the rim. The canoes ranged in size from 3.5 to 12 m. The largest ones held over 20 men and were used on large lakes and big rivers. Smaller canoes held two or three people and were used on journeys where portages were frequent.

The women made twine from the inner bark of elm trees. They cut the bark into narrow strips, then boiled them in ashes and water so the strips would separate into threads. Men wove the threads into fishnets. Women made the threads into beautiful burden straps up to 5 m long. They braided the bark threads, then laid several braids beside each other and knitted them together with needles made of bone. The women wore such straps around their heads to help them support the weight of cradleboards, food baskets, or other burdens packed on wooden frames, which were like the frames of modern backpacks.

Men playing snowsnake. Both players and spectators often bet valued possessions, including weapons, tools, jewellery and clothing, on the outcome of the game.

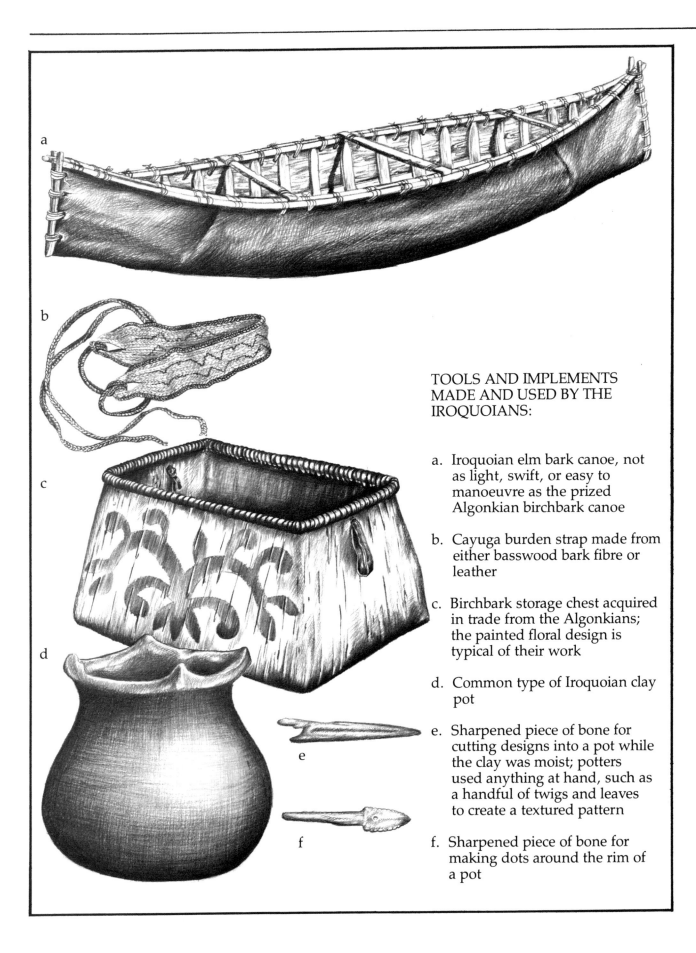

TOOLS AND IMPLEMENTS MADE AND USED BY THE IROQUOIANS:

a. Iroquoian elm bark canoe, not as light, swift, or easy to manoeuvre as the prized Algonkian birchbark canoe

b. Cayuga burden strap made from either basswood bark fibre or leather

c. Birchbark storage chest acquired in trade from the Algonkians; the painted floral design is typical of their work

d. Common type of Iroquoian clay pot

e. Sharpened piece of bone for cutting designs into a pot while the clay was moist; potters used anything at hand, such as a handful of twigs and leaves to create a textured pattern

f. Sharpened piece of bone for making dots around the rim of a pot

Social and Political Structure

The Iroquoian nations formed leagues because they wanted peace with their neighbours and trading partners, and allies to fight against common foes. The League of the Iroquois, the most famous one, was started over 500 years ago and still meets today. The Iroquois believe their league was founded by their ancestors Hiawatha and Dekaniwedah. Hiawatha's name means "he who seeks the wampum belt"; he was a different Hiawatha from the one in the famous poem by Henry Wadsworth Longfellow.

Hiawatha was an Onondaga whose family was killed in a blood feud. He grieved so much that he turned into a cannibal monster, consuming himself with anger and sadness. Wandering in exile, he reached a lake. As he stood on its shore, the sky filled with wild ducks. Landing on the water's surface, the ducks drank and preened, soaking their feathers in the water, until the lake was dry. Hiawatha saw small spiral shells on the lake bottom. To mark his grief, he picked up the shells and threaded them on the stalks of bulrushes.

Dekaniwedah, "the master of things," part god and part human, appeared. He told Hiawatha that he would help him to form a league of nations to prevent blood feuds and to spare people the terrible sadness of losing loved ones. The two travelled in a white canoe throughout the lands of the Iroquois, inviting the nations to join together in peace. The Mohawk were

Hiawatha picking up wampum shells from the bottom of the dried-up lake

Top: the ten long strings of white wampum used in the great council
Bottom: the tally-stick and white wampum sent to all the member nations of a league to summon them to the great council meeting

the first to join, so they became known as "the elder brothers."

The Iroquois saw their league as having the same form as their homes. Like a huge longhouse, it was said to contain many fires, one for each tribal family. The people were to live together in peace, like one clan.

The constitution of the league later became a model for the constitution of the United States. All people had freedom of speech, freedom of religion and the right to hunt on the lands of member tribes. No Iroquois could shed the blood of any other Iroquois. If violence did occur, the victim (or the victim's family) had to be compensated by the payment of white wampum or goods to a value set by the league or tribal council. Witchcraft, treason and theft were crimes, and those who kept breaking the laws could be exiled. Exile meant that the guilty person was forced to leave the tribe. He or she would no longer have a home or family and, therefore, no protection or support. This punishment may seem harsh to us, but it was necessary in a society without jails, where co-operation was vital to the good of the people.

The constitution also set out the powers and responsibilities of the league, nation and village. The highest level, the great council of the league, was similar to Canada's parliament or the United States' congress. The tribal council was like a provincial legislature, and the village council was like a city council. However, at all these levels, representatives were chosen by the clans, not by voters living in the same area.

On the great council were 50 sachems or peace chiefs. Each nation had a different number of sachems on the council, but the numbers did not reflect the power of the nations in the league. The numbers depended on the agreements made when the nations joined the league and on the number of clans in each tribe. The nations with the most sachems could not control the council, since each nation had only one vote. The sachems from each nation had to agree on how to use their vote.

Once a year, the great council met in the land of the Onondaga, who were the "keepers of the council fire." They summoned the sachems to the meeting by sending messengers to the neighbouring Oneida and Cayuga. Each messenger carried a tally-stick with strings of wampum attached to it. The number of notches on the stick showed how many days it would be until the meeting. The Oneida sent a similar message to the nearby Mohawk, and the Cayuga sent one to their neighbours, the Seneca.

The great council made new laws and dealt with problems that concerned all the member nations. Each meeting lasted several days. Because all the sachems had to agree on each final decision, they made very long and eloquent speeches in order to try to convince the others of the rightness of their point of view. As each sachem spoke, he held strings of wampum in his hand to show that his words were true. When the wampum was taken from him and passed to the next speaker, it was a sign that the truth of his words was accepted.

A sachem served on the council for his whole life, unless he was removed by the matron of his clan. When a sachem died, the clan matron consulted with the other women in her group and chose a

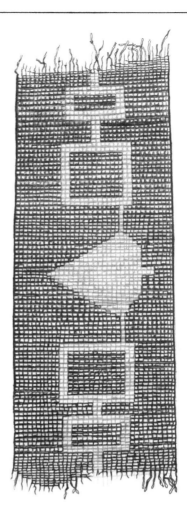

The Hiawatha wampum belt, commemorating the founding of the League of the Iroquois

replacement. Her choice was voted on by all the adult members of the clan. If he was approved, the new sachem took on the name and position of the former sachem.

Tribal councils included the sachems, the war chiefs and often the clan matrons. War chiefs were chosen by their clans for their courage and skill in warfare. The meetings were open to all members of the tribe. They had no vote but could influence decisions by making speeches. Tribal councils dealt with trade and warfare between their tribe and nations outside their league, and with crimes and punishments within their tribe.

Great council meeting of the five nations of the League of the Iroquois; the Mohawk speaker holds the wampum belt of unity while he addresses the council

Village councils usually included respected elders (both men and women), clan chiefs and matrons. Councils reached decisions through discussion and agreement. They co-ordinated village projects, kept order in the village, decided on compensation that wrong-doers should pay their victims, and set dates for rituals, ceremonies, dances and games.

The clan system gave the people a voice in all levels of government. The same clans could be found in several nations in each league. Members of one nation who were travelling through the lands of another tribe were treated as family members by people who belonged to their clan. This linked the nations in a league together.

Farming and Food

Cultivated fields lay outside every village. Land for farming was cleared by the men, who girdled all the trees in an area and waited until they died. This made it much easier to burn them as an aid to cutting them down with stone axes. Stumps were burned, and the roots were left to dry before being removed. Then the women levelled the ground around the remains of stumps with large, hook-shaped wooden rakes.

At planting time, the women soaked the seeds of corn (saved from the previous year's crop) in water to make them ready to sprout. The women in a clan worked together to help plant each other's fields. They used small wooden spades to form the soil into broad mounds about 30 cm high. Nine or ten holes were poked in the top of each mound, and seeds were planted in them. The mounds protected the seeds from the cold and discouraged weeds. In the same fields as the corn, many different kinds of beans were grown, especially kidney and lima beans.

Sunflowers were grown for the oil in their seeds, which was used for cooking. People also rubbed the oil on their bodies for protection from the cold or sun, and to soothe cuts or wounds.

Pumpkin, melon and squash seeds were sprouted in trays spread with light soil, then were moved outside and planted in the fields. In most tribes, tobacco was grown in small gardens. It was the only

Seneca method of braiding together ears of corn into a bunch for drying

crop grown by men, who used it in ceremonies.

As the crops grew, little girls worked beside their mothers and aunts to weed the rows of plants. At harvest time, some women picked the ears of corn and put them into baskets. Others carried the full baskets to the longhouses. A third group cooked for the workers. The work was joyous, as the food supply for the winter was being made secure. In rest periods, they sang, played gambling games and told stories. At night, men worked with the women to bind the ears of corn into bundles which they hung from the roof beams of each longhouse.

When the corn was dry, the women and girls scraped the kernels off the cobs with a tool made out of a deer jaw. The dried corn was stored in bark casks. Beans were dried and kept in bark containers with lids. Squash and pumpkins were placed in deep, bark-lined pits in the houses, then covered with earth.

Women also gathered wild plums, grapes, cherries, berries and sweet crab apples. They picked many wild nuts including chestnuts, black walnuts and hickory nuts. Maple sap, gathered in the spring, was the only sweetener. This liquid was stored in seamless bark containers made in the shape of boats.

Men brought the clan its fish and meat. The Huron caught trout, sturgeon and whitefish in Georgian Bay, paddling their canoes 5 km out from shore to set their nets. Other Iroquoian nations relied less on fish than the Huron, as game was more abundant in their lands. The forests were home to black bears, elk, deer, rabbits and wolves, which were shot with bows and

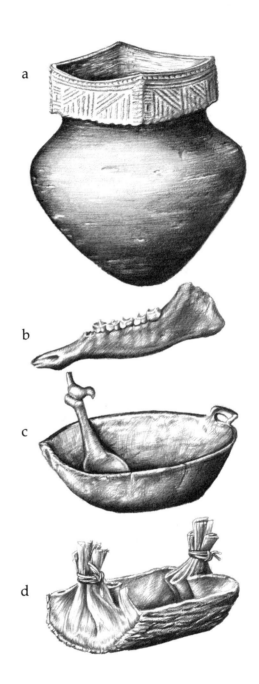

a. Clay cooking pot

b. Deer jaw scraper for removing dried kernels from the cob

c. Oneida wooden bowl for preparing or serving food or medicine

d. Seneca elm bark container for water or maple sap

arrows or caught in traps and snares.

To make a snare, a young tree was bent down and attached to the ground with a loop that would catch an animal by its hind legs. When a creature stepped into the loop, the tree was released and sprang up, suspending the catch in midair.

Game birds were plentiful. Wild turkeys, geese, ducks, herons, pigeons and partridges were caught in large nets hung between two trees. As many as 200 fowl a night could be captured this way, enough to feed all the people in a large village.

The clan's food stores were controlled by the women. When they felt that a war should not be fought, they prevented the men from going by refusing to provide food for the journey. If council meetings were not proceeding as they wished, they refused to prepare meals for the councillors.

A woman cooked food for her own family at the fireplace closest to her section of the longhouse. Water was boiled by dropping heated stones into a clay pot full of water. For slower cooking, the clay pots were hung directly over the fire.

Dried corn was prepared by boiling it first in water to which wood ashes were added. The lye in the ashes made the kernels swell and lose their hulls. The corn was then washed and cooked in soup with kidney beans, meat or boiled fish.

Men and women work together to clear the land and prepare new fields for planting. On the left, a man is chopping down a girdled, dead tree. On the right, men are building a small lodge out of saplings and bark for use as a shelter or storage.

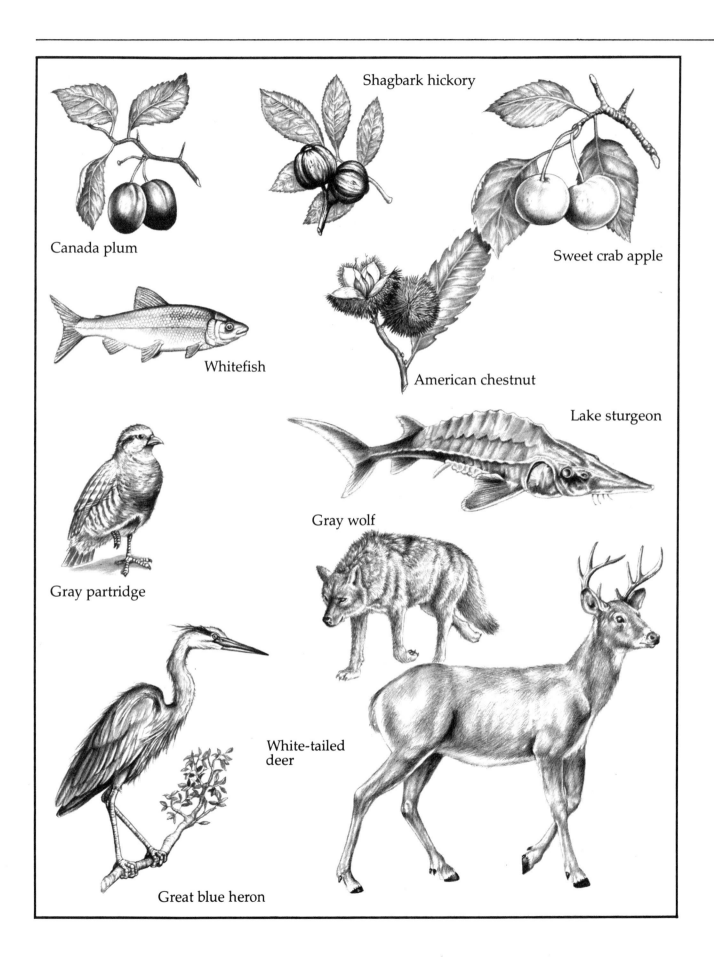

Shagbark hickory

Canada plum

Sweet crab apple

American chestnut

Whitefish

Lake sturgeon

Gray partridge

Gray wolf

White-tailed deer

Great blue heron

Corn was also ground into meal and used to make a sort of bread. The loaves were small and flat, about 4 cm thick and 15 cm long. Sometimes dried berries or nuts were put in the bread. The loaves were boiled in water in large pots.

Most households ate only one large meal a day, usually in the late morning, though food was always available. Food was served from the pots with stone or wooden ladles. People ate with wooden or bark spoons from wooden bowls and drank from cups made of turtle shells or carved from wood.

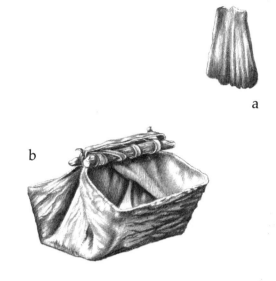

a

b

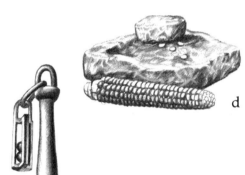

c

d

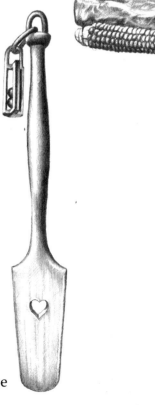

TOOLS USED FOR CULTIVATING CROPS AND PREPARING FOOD:

a. Hoe blade made from an antler

b. Seneca double-pocketed elm bark basket to hold seeds for planting

c. Seneca husking pin

d. Seneca stone mortar and grinder

e. Wooden paddle for stirring soup

e

Clothing

Clothing serves as both protection and a form of decoration. The Iroquoians wore many kinds of clothing, all of it made from animal hides and furs. Women prepared the hides by removing the hair and flesh with stone scrapers. Then they soaked the hides in a solution of boiled deer brains to soften them. After drying, the hides were smoked to make them durable. Pieces of leather were cut to shape and sewn together with sinew that was threaded through holes pierced by bone awls. Skins of beaver, bobcat and squirrel were scraped only on the inside, leaving on the fur for warmth and decoration.

In summer, men and women wore loincloths of soft deerskin, held in place by a thong tied around the waist. Huron women also wore a skirt that reached almost to the knee. Both sexes often left their bodies bare from the waist up. They all wore moccasins on their feet.

When more protection was needed because of cold weather, men wore kilts and women wore longer skirts. Both sexes also wore leggings and jerkins with sleeves. These were held in place with leather thongs or burden straps tied around the body. In winter, they wore cloaks or robes made from bear, deer, buffalo or beaver skins.

They painted their bodies with geometrical designs or pictures of people and animals, which usually had a religious meaning. The paint was made by mixing natural pigments such as red ochre,

Man's summer clothing made of buckskin

Woman's summer dress made of buckskin

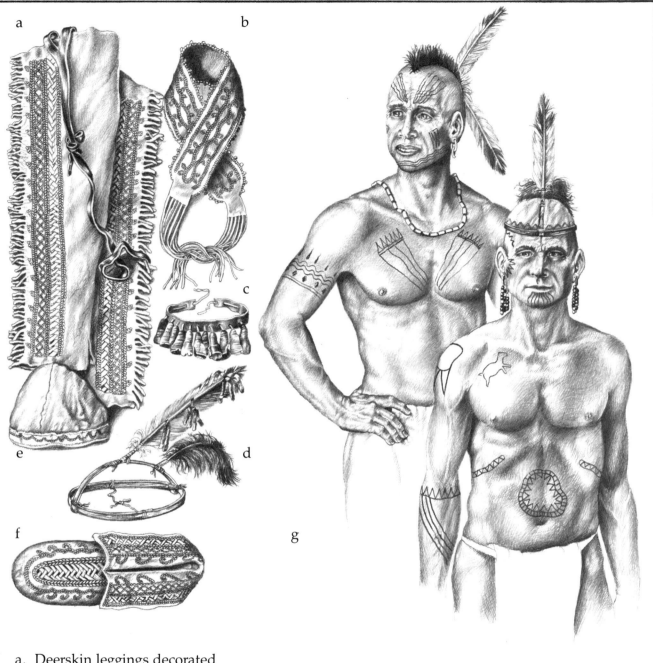

a. Deerskin leggings decorated with dyed porcupine quills

b. Deerskin shoulder strap or waist belt

c. Rattle made out of deer hooves worn strapped to the knee of a false face dancer

d. Seneca headdress of wood splints topped with eagle feathers

e. Deerskin cap placed inside the headdress

f. Man's moccasin decorated with dyed porcupine quills

g. Painted body designs, adapted from a painting called ''The Death of Wolfe'' by Benjamin West (1738-1820) bloodroot and charcoal with sunflower seed oil. The Neutral and Tobacco inserted the pigments under their skin to produce permanent tattoos.

Iroquoians liked to wear ornaments such as woven sashes, fur and feather neckpieces, and feathered caps. They embroidered their clothing with dyed moosehair and porcupine quills. Everyday jewellery was made from common materials: feathers were made into earrings, animal teeth were hung as pendants on thongs, and segments of bone were strung into necklaces. On special occasions, both men and women wore bracelets and necklaces made from shell beads. Shells acquired in trade were a sign of wealth. Women also wore large shell plaques over their stomachs. A woman might wear as much as 5 kg of shell ornaments.

Hair styles were another important form of decoration. Women usually wore their hair hanging down the back in a single braid, bound with a thong. Men's styles varied. Iroquois warriors favoured the scalplock — a lock of hair dangling down the back of the neck — with the hair on the head shaved except for a strip down the middle from the forehead to the scalplock. Some wore close-fitting caps with a feather attached to the back. Huron men liked rolls of hair over their ears, or one side of the hair worn long and the other shaved. Some Huron men wore headbands made of snakeskin, with the snake's tail hanging down the back.

After contact with European traders, Iroquoians began to use woollen cloth rather than animal skins for their clothing. They embroidered these clothes with small glass trade beads in elaborate flower designs.

MAN'S WINTER OUTFIT: leggings, breechclout, kilt, moccasins and cloak

Beliefs and Ceremonies

Iroquoian people believed in many spirit forces created by a supreme being. Sky spirit forces took the form of wind, thunder, sun, moon and stars. Earth spirits took the form of plants and animals. All the spirit forces together were called "orenda," the Mohawk word for "song." Like a song, spirit forces flowed through all nature and controlled the weather and the lives of people, animals and plants.

They believed that anything they dreamed had to happen. If a warrior dreamed about being wounded, he would ask a friend to cut him slightly so that the dream would come true in this harmless way, rather than in battle. The shaman or medicine man dreamed more than an ordinary person and used the spirit forces that came to him in dreams to cure illness.

Each village had a special longhouse where councils and ceremonies were held. Many of the ceremonies were like plays, in which songs, speeches and dances told a story. The eagle dance tells the story of a boy who was carried off by the giant dew eagle, a powerful spirit bird. The boy returned to earth as a man with the power to cure illness. The bird was called the dew eagle because it collected a pool of dew in the hollow between its shoulders. When the thunder spirits that normally brought rain failed to come, the dew eagle showered the earth with dew to water the crops. The bird's power brought help for both sick people and plants.

Two of the four men taking part in the Seneca eagle dance

In the eagle dance, four young men from two different clans danced like eagles, while singers chanted and beat small drums carved from tree burls. The drums were filled with water and covered with ground-hog hide. The water gave the drums a high, clear tone. The dancers bent down to pick up small objects in their mouths in imitation of eagles feeding. Each held a horn rattle in his right hand to imitate the sound of birds scratching, and a feather fan in his left hand to represent wings with the power to sweep away evil. The sounds made by the rattles, drums and human voices helped people to contact the spirit forces.

Tobacco was often used in ceremonies because its smoke was thought to rise up to heaven, taking prayers with it. Tobacco was thrown directly on hot coals to produce smoke, or smoked in stone or clay pipes. Pipes were smoked with honoured guests, to end disputes or to strengthen friendships between tribes. The pipes were not passed from person to person as they were among the plains tribes.

Every year the Iroquoians held six or eight festivals. The most important was the midwinter festival. They feasted, played games, sang, danced, prayed and made speeches. They also gave thanks to the spirits of their most important food crops — corn, beans and squash — which they thought of as three sisters who were daughters of the mother earth. Other festivals celebrated the time of planting corn, the time when the corn was green, and the harvest of corn and other crops. They also celebrated the season when sap flowed in the maple trees, and the season when berries ripened. By watching the

A dreamer, carving a false face mask from a living tree, is chipping flint to make a carving tool

False face dancers driving out the evil spirits that cause sickness

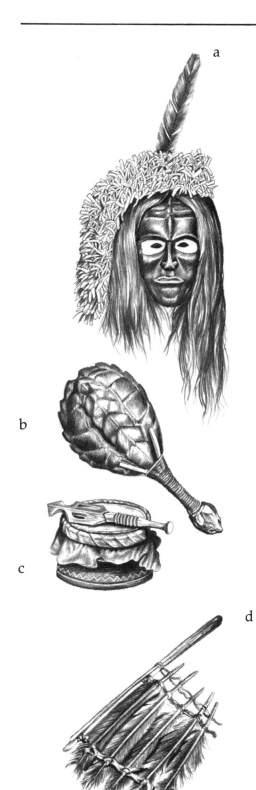

stars, they knew when to begin their festivals and when to plant and harvest crops.

Special ceremonies were put on by societies made up of people who had dreamed of the same spirit forces. One of these was the False Face Society, whose members were believed to have the power to drive out the evil spirits that caused illness. A man was called to membership in the society if a false face spirit came to him in a dream. He was accepted into it after he carved a mask to represent the spirit he had seen. The mask was carved into a living tree to give it the tree's power to heal itself. When the finished mask was cut out of the tree, it came alive with the power to heal sickness. Every spring and fall, false face dancers wore their masks and raided every longhouse. They crawled, jumped, hopped and struck the floor with turtle shell rattles. While they danced, they screamed and groaned. They had to be even more frightening than the evil spirits in order to drive out illness.

CEREMONIAL OBJECTS:

a. False face mask representing the spirit of the harvest

b. Turtle shell rattle used in the false face ceremony

c. Burl drum filled with water, used in the eagle dance

d. Five-feathered fan used in the eagle dance

e. Horn rattle used in the eagle dance

Trade

The men of all the Iroquoian-speaking nations engaged in trade with other nations in their leagues and with friendly neighbouring tribes. The Huron were the most successful traders since they were located on important canoe routes. Their territory was also particularly suitable for growing corn, so they grew a surplus to trade for meat and other foods which were scarce near their villages. They also got tools, clothing and ornaments. Huron traders were careful to maintain good relations with their trading partners. They often invited them to feasts and exchanged children with them to guarantee friendship.

Trading parties left Huron villages from early spring through summer and went out in every direction. A small group might consist of eight men travelling in two canoes. Large groups with up to a dozen big canoes, each carrying as many as 20 men, could travel as far as Lakes Michigan and Superior. The sachems of the Huron League decided how many young men should be allowed to travel, for some had to stay behind to protect their villages from enemy raiders.

From the Erie and Neutral to the south, the Huron got raccoon-skin robes, bobcat pelts, wampum, conch shells and calcium carbonate stones used in healing rites, and gourds in which to store oil. The shells may have come north from the Gulf of Mexico, in trade from tribe to tribe. From the Algonkian-speaking tribes to the north,

Huron trader exchanging dried corn for furs from an Algonkian hunter

the Huron got furs, dried fish, warm clothing and birchbark canoes. These canoes were prized because they were lighter and swifter than the Iroquoian canoes made of elm bark, for birch trees were scarce in Iroquoian territory. From the Cree who lived in the northern forest, the Huron got medicinal herbs and amulets. And from tribes living along Lake Superior and Lake Michigan, they got flint to make into tools, and copper. Copper was a rare metal, too soft to be made into tools, so it was used for ornaments in much the same way that we use gold today.

The Iroquois travelled and traded more on foot than by canoe. Their trading links with the Algonkian tribes were not as well established as those of the Huron. Their main trading partners were the Susquehannok and Delaware to the south, from whom they got shells. The Iroquois then traded some shells to the Neutral and Petun for tobacco and northern products received from the Huron. Because they had good access to shells from the coast, the Iroquois often used wampum as a form of money in exchange for goods.

Direct trade between the Iroquois and Huron did take place when there was peace, but the feuds between the two leagues made it unreliable.

In the early days of the fur trade, the Huron came to be important middlemen between the northern forest tribes and European traders. The Huron got furs from the Algonkians and traded them to the Europeans for metal tomahawks, metal knives, guns, glass beads and woollen cloth. The Iroquois traded beaver pelts from their own territory to Europeans in exchange for the same goods.

Iroquois with a burden frame secured to his back by means of a burden strap passed across his chest; for heavier loads he would also use an additional strap across his forehead

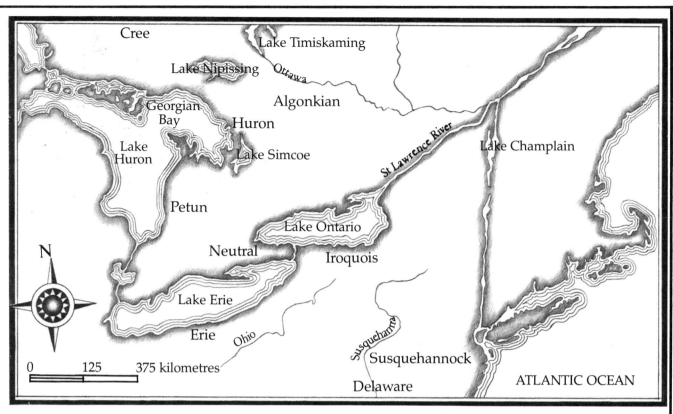

TRADING PARTNERS OF THE
IROQUOIANS AND THE WATER
SYSTEMS USED AS TRADE
ROUTES

a. Perforated wampum shells used
   as decoration and as a form of
   money for trade

b. Iroquois snowshoe made of
   hickory wood and laced with
   deerskin thongs

c. Burden frame with strap made
   of either bark fibre or deerskin

d. Algonkian birchbark canoe, a
   prized trade item

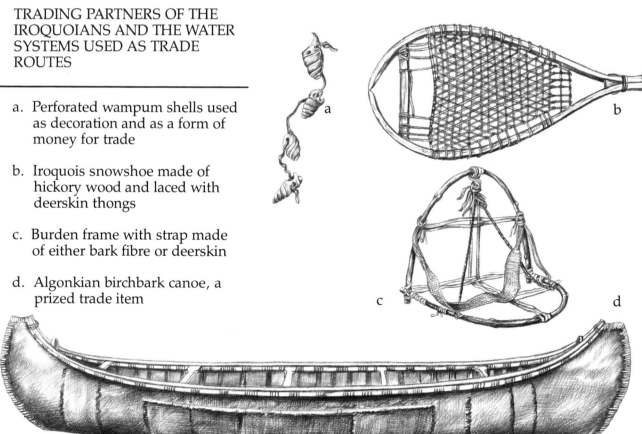

War and Peace

Being a warrior was important to a young Iroquoian man because raiding enemy villages gave him a chance to show courage, strength and knowledge of distant places. An older man, however, was more often called upon to become a sachem and showed his wisdom and diplomacy by leading councils for peace. Each showed good qualities in his own way.

Europeans fought wars to capture territory, gain trade or contest religious differences. But the Iroquoians fought blood feuds in which revenge and honour were more important than conquest. They made quick raids into enemy territory instead of fighting long battles.

A blood feud began when a person from one nation killed someone from a nation belonging to another league. It was a matter of honour to avenge the death by killing or capturing someone from the killer's nation or village. Until they did so, people in the victim's village felt weak and in danger.

Most raids took place between nations of different leagues. Raids were made only during the summer when swift travel was possible, as war parties often travelled long distances to raid an enemy village. Each warrior carried a bag of roasted corn meal mixed with maple sugar that would feed him for six to eight weeks on the trail. This trail food could be eaten by itself, or be cooked with fish and game caught during the journey.

Huron warrior wearing armour made from slats of wood

Until the Europeans gave them guns and metal tomahawks, warriors fought with clubs that had a round stone set into a carved wooden handle. They also used bows and arrows. The men made their own bows, which were over a metre long, out of wood. They hardened the wood with fire and shaped the bow with a shell knife. The bows, strung with deer sinew or cord made from hemp, required great strength to bend. Arrows were nearly a metre long, with a flint arrowhead at one end, and feathers twisted and tied at the other to make them revolve in flight. This gave their arrows much greater speed and accuracy than European arrows had at that time.

Warriors protected their bodies with shields made of wicker or bark, covered with hide. Some warriors, including the Huron, used light armour made from thin slats of wood, woven together with deerskin thongs. The shields and body armour were tough and flexible enough to stop stone-tipped arrows and deflect the blows of stone-headed clubs. They were also light enough to be carried over long distances. Often, warriors wore their finest shell necklaces and other ornaments on a raid. If pursued too closely they would drop these treasures and escape, while their enemies stopped to pick them up.

The greatest proof of a warrior's power was to bring back captives to his village. People believed that once an enemy was in their power, they regained the strength lost when their relative had been killed. Captives were often tortured in order to make their strength part of the strength of the village, rather than as punishment. A prisoner who was to be tortured and killed was allowed to give a feast in honour of his

Old Seneca sachem holding a pipe and peace council wampum

Iroquois warrior putting the final touches to the bow he is making from hickory wood

own death. The feast was sponsored by the family whose relative had been killed.

If a prisoner reminded his captors of the dead relative, they might spare his life and give him the name and titles of the man he replaced. Such an adopted prisoner might even join a war party against his own people since, by being captured, he would have lost honour among them.

The great council met to discuss disputes between league nations and to make peace with nations of other leagues. As a peace offering, each sachem smoked his own pipe and threw tobacco into the fire. Peace was often brought about because of great speeches in which a sachem would sing and act out many of his points. There were also special dances for making peace between feuding nations. At the conclusion of peace talks, representatives of warring nations exchanged presents such as shell ornaments, wampum and furs as a sign of goodwill.

WEAPONS OF WAR AND SYMBOLS OF PEACE

a. Cayuga bow

b. War club made from ironwood and a round stone

c. Wooden arrow with flint arrowhead and twisted feathers

d. Buckskin quiver to hold arrows

e. Shoulder bag for food, decorated with dyed porcupine quills and moosehair on black buckskin, probably Huron

f. Onondaga national wampum belt; the design represents an ever-growing tree to symbolize the perpetuity of the league

g. Wampum belt to summon the clan council to a meeting

h. Clay pipes used in ceremonies

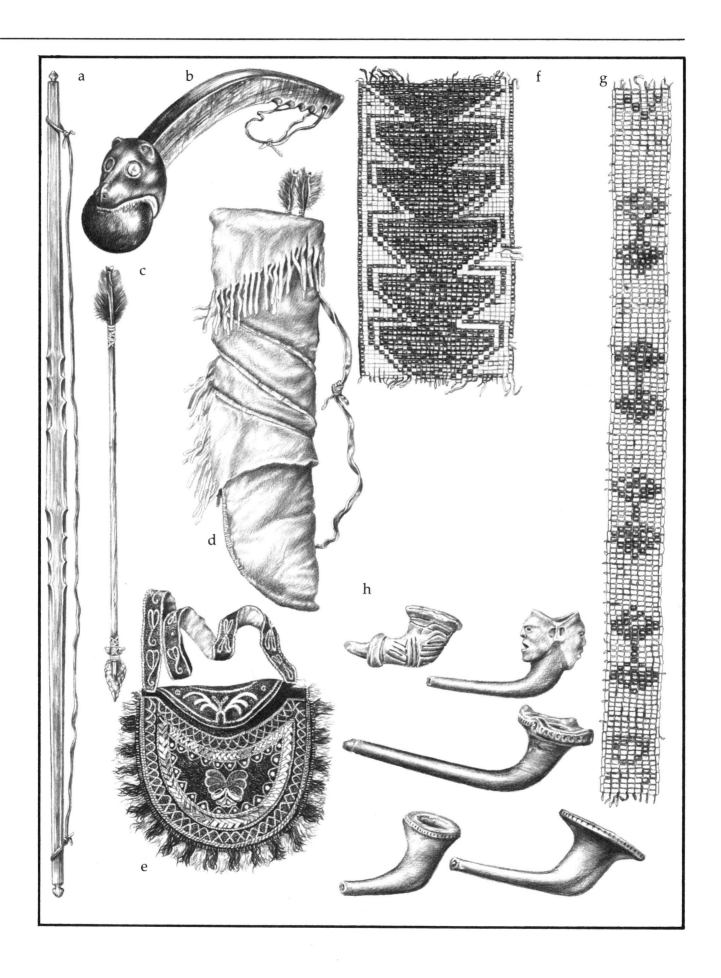

a b c d e f g h

After the Europeans Came

In 1534, the French explorer Jacques Cartier saw corn growing along the banks of the St. Lawrence River, near the present-day city of Montreal. He was the first European to discover the prosperous farming territory of the Iroquoian people. After him came explorers, traders and missionaries who wished to bring European civilization to the native people, but whose presence actually brought about terrible destruction.

Thousands of native people died in epidemics of smallpox and other European diseases. And the bitter competition in the fur trade led to increased warfare among the Iroquoian leagues.

The Iroquois soon killed off most of the beaver in their territory and began raiding Huron villages for furs. In the winter of 1649, large Iroquois war parties invaded Huron territory. Only a few of the Huron survived the attack that followed.

The Five Nations of the League of the Iroquois became the Six Nations in 1722 when the Tuscarora joined. They fought in many more wars, the last in 1776 when the American colonies declared independence from Britain. The Seneca, Cayuga, Onondaga and Mohawk were persuaded to join the British, but the Oneida and Tuscarora joined the Americans. Thus, the long peace among the nations of the League of the Iroquois was broken by a war that really had nothing to do with them.

After the British lost the war, Joseph Brant, a Mohawk leader with a college education, led his people into southern Ontario. They settled on a reserve at Grand River, near the town of Brantford, since named for their leader. Other Mohawks established reserves at St. Regis on the St. Lawrence River, and Caughnawaga near Montreal.

The Iroquois nations that stayed in American territory had a difficult life. In 1800, a religious leader named Handsome Lake began to persuade his Seneca people to give up fighting and learn to use horses and plows. He received his power from dreams and visions. Many Iroquois still follow his teachings and meet in modern longhouses where they repeat his speeches from memory. They call themselves "The Longhouse People."

In the early 1900s, Mohawks at Caughnawaga began to work on high steel construction projects such as bridges and skyscrapers. They liked the work because it called for the same keen sight, courage and co-ordination that their ancestors valued. They are famous for their skill and bravery in this dangerous occupation.

Today, Iroquois people live on reserves in Ontario, Quebec and New York State. Many still think of themselves as a united people, so they believe they have the right to cross the Canada-United States border without restriction.

The Iroquois great council still meets, and the clan matrons still appoint sachems, but modern leaders such as band chiefs are elected. Members of the False Face Society continue to dance wearing their masks, in order to bring about good health for their people. The Iroquois are proud of a rich history that began long before the Europeans came to their country.

Joseph Brant, adapted from the portrait of him by the English artist Romney